About the author

I grew up in a small town on the central coast of California. Here I spent most of my childhood playing sports and loving nature. School was easy and I got along well with everyone. I love people. I've been good with words and poetry has always been a great way for me to express my feelings. As a profession, I am in the medical field as a radiology technologist. With this career I have been around a lot of hurt and have been able to help with the healing process. Since then, I have fallen in love with the idea of healing. Whether emotional or physical, this world needs it on every level. I will help to facilitate that need on a grand scale someday.

I have been married to my wonderful wife, Amber, for almost five years. We have a three-year-old named Hazel and a baby on the way, named Pearl. I couldn't be prouder. We have a house in the country with five chickens, two dogs, and a pig. I am a very blessed man.

INSPIRED INSPIRATIONS

SETH M KOLACH

INSPIRED INSPIRATIONS

Vanguard Press

VANGUARD PAPERBACK

© Copyright 2021
Seth M Kolach

The right of Seth M Kolach to be identified as author of this work has been asserted by him in accordance with the Copyright, Designs and Patents Act 1988.

All Rights Reserved

No reproduction, copy or transmission of this publication may be made without written permission.
No paragraph of this publication may be reproduced, copied or transmitted save with the written permission of the publisher, or in accordance with the provisions of the Copyright Act 1956 (as amended).

Any person who commits any unauthorised act in relation to this publication may be liable to criminal prosecution and civil claims for damages.

A CIP catalogue record for this title is available from the British Library.

ISBN 978 1 800160 98 9

Vanguard Press is an imprint of
Pegasus Elliot MacKenzie Publishers Ltd.
www.pegasuspublishers.com

First Published in 2021

Vanguard Press
Sheraton House Castle Park
Cambridge England

Printed & Bound in Great Britain

Dedication

I would like to dedicate this book to my family and friends. You all have always supported me and been there for me through everything. I believe we are a product of our environment and you created a great one to grow. Thank you.

Contents

Inspired Inspirations 13
Me 14
I Am Healing 19
Revealization 21
Flying 22
Night Dance 24
Sunshine 25
I Am Affirmations 27
Change Your Thoughts 29
It Is 31
Forgiveness 33
Lights 35
Trauma 37
Fear Not to Love 39
His Will 41
I Am 43
True Dreams 45
Bad and Good 47
Breath Deep 49
Patience 51
Hold On 53
Alcohol 55

- Away I Lift 57
- Grow Slow 59
- I Love You God 62
- Reality 64
- Staying Awake 68
- Just for You 71
- Meditation 74
- Abundance 76
- Changes 78
- Judgment 81
- 5:55 83
- Mother Spirt Ayahuasca 86
- Music 89
- Love 92
- Collective Consciousness Shift 94
- Love Inspired 96
- Sedona 98
- Akashic Record 100
- Death 103
- Changes 106
- MLK Dreams a dream 109
- One 111
- Love and Light 112
- Life Ripple 114

Wake Up 115
Be Grey 118
Remove the Veil 121
Mind's Eye 123
Go Within 125
Wake up 127
2020 Visions 130

Inspired Inspirations

In spirit with enthusiasm for the source
Envelopes my body with magnetic force
Being silent and by listening
The words flow out, with their meanings glistening
Becoming aware and consciously awake
Makes me want to give these words for mankind's sake
Give these words for you to do as you need
Hopefully, inside they will plant a seed
Let it grow and watch you become the change
See your world around you rearrange
Continue to learn and grow
Seek inner peace and the outer will glow
Be okay with what will happen
That is when you will start to tap in
Be aware of your thoughts
Our minds are powerful and call the shots
I hope these words find you well
And speak into your bodies, every cell
Let's be the collective consciousness for a better world on earth
Join the world in a spiritual rebirth

Me

I was born Easter Sunday, April 7th 1985
At seven a.m. my soul took my body for a test drive
That day in Santa Barbara, I was adopted at birth
To join my loving parents on this wild earth
I was introduced to my older adopted bro
Brought to a loving home where I could learn and grow
Paso Robles was the town I raised
And as I grew, sporting events filled my days
I would swim, play soccer, basketball, and run
Baseball, football, and triathlons for fun
My dad was always there, helping to guide me
He was great coach and took a lot of pride in me
I got good grades and loved to make people laugh
I was always up to pull a good gaffe
I liked girls from a very early age
And loved nothing more than to be on the big stage
When I was young, I got in trouble and did some dumb things
And I'm pretty sure I wore out my guardian angel's wings

I graduated high school and tried my hand at
baseball in college
Baseball didn't work out, so I stuck with the
knowledge
Ended up back in Santa Barbara in a radiology
program
Still trying to learn about this person I am
I partied a lot, but always got the work done
Had a lot of friends and sure had a lot of fun
Broke some hearts and had my heart broke the
same
At that age, was any one really to blame
I ended up working at my place of birth
Doing CT scans on people getting hurt on this
earth
I learned a lot of skills and loved helping the
community
But noticed that medicine was sometimes, out of
whack with unity
If money is more important than one's health
Then people will die because of their wealth
I will open a healing center one day
All facets of healing, where no one's turned away
I worked there as long as I could afford
And just like my birth at Cottage, I cut the cord
I moved back home to buy a house
And then went on the search for a loving spouse

I met my wife on a dating site
Everything about her just felt right
We got married not much longer after
And now have a four-year-old daughter who is full of laughter
We live in a beautiful home out of town
Where my family and friends are close around
Speaking of family, I've met my biological side
I even got to see my half-sister become a bride
I have given thanks to my birth mom and dad for what they did
It must have been hard to give away your kid
But they did the right thing in a very tough spot
And she was able to give my soul a vessel and give my life a shot
I now do X-ray at a local state prison
It's funny how prison rhymes with risen
I was raised Christian and we went to church as kids
There are a lot of good teachings and a lot of forbids
I took what I learned and used the knowledge to grow
And I started to seek God, because you reap what you sow
If you ask you shall be given
I started asking about this life I've been living

If you seek you will find
God will start to put things straight into your mind
Knock and the door will open
Don't stop believing and never stop hoping
I had a spiritual awakening and a better understanding of God
I learned so much, so fast, I was truly awed
I studied countless videos and online text
I finished one and it was on to the next
I was so excited I tried to share with people that were close
My adopted mom was the one that understood the most
She was going through the very same thing
And we had no idea what this world could bring
My adopted mom has always shown me wrong from right
She is and has always been my beacon of light
I credit her for who I am
Always listening and helping me to be a better man
I feel alive since this has happened and wanted to share
And put the words to poetry to express how I care
We are all perfect in the eyes of the Lord
I hope my poems to you, are a harmonious chord
I am not done doing things for mankind

It's what this life is all about, you will find
So, take what I say with a grain of salt
And seek the truth for yourself and God will open his vault
I love you all and I wish you the best
Now go and seek, God will take care of the rest

I Am Healing

I sit and imagine a healing center for all
With the words I AM HEALING, high up on the wall
With wonderful aromas of incense wafting through
A place to heal for me and you

People practicing yoga on the lawn
An open-air prayer room, open from dusk till dawn
Speakers coming to give their healing words of peace
A place where disease and hurt will become deceased

Reiki, massage, acupuncture, and sound healings
Wind chimes, mantras, herbal remedies and good feelings
Friendly people with the same goal in mind
One's healthy birthright, we shall find

Shamans, pastors, mediums, all working as one
United together until the work is done
Changing the conscious minds of the community

To be an example for the world, that's in need of
unity

We all may not all believe in the same
But believing in healing will be our claim to fame
We will give back, what we have been given
And we will forgive those who have not been
forgiven

Imagine a place to come to heal
Where there is no judgment, only good feelings to
feel
A place for all to go get back aligned
For now, this place is only in my mind

But I believe that it will happen some day
And I give it to God to show me the way
I will not stop believing in this
Until the I Am Healing center, does exist

Revealization

Take this vail from over our eyes
Lift the darkness and the lies
Clear the path and show me the way
Reveal to me the words, you meant to say
The I am, that you are, is I
The eternal being of the most high
Rid us from this pain and strife
I am a branch from your forever tree of life
Open the eyes of the blinded
Give them the sight that they too may find it
Reconnect our connectiveness with love
Show us what this universe is really made of
Teach us to communicate with spirit
Help us to realize that you always hear it
Cast away doubt and let confidence reign
I am health, happy, and sane
Spiritual beings learning on the earth
Death is nothing other than our souls' rebirth
Help others, help you, to help others
My sisters, brothers, fathers, and mothers

Flying

I close my eyes and take internal flight

The bright lights dim and it's dark as night

Then the light begins to reappear

And the sounds of guitar, I begin to hear

I float now, not feeling the weight

I love now, not feeling the hate

Drifting off into an ever-expansive place

That can only be described as an amazing grace

Voices sing in harmony

And I realize that it's all for me

My soul has taken flight

Clothed in a bright white light

I am my soul and my soul are I

This must be what it's like, when I die

Eternal bliss in a place filled with love

An eternity of life from above

I enjoy this vacation from reality

Saying goodbye, I head back home to me

I return my soul to its earthly dwelling

Because here is where it does the excelling.

Night Dance

The slumber of man at night is far more profound
To seek infinite knowledge from another realm
Bathing in the vast subconscious of the universe
Dreaming a reality of its own
In another place, in another zone

Gifts of God are bestowed on man during rest
Dreams come to those who are aligned
Visions that manifest gold upon our hands
To be used to better man
This is God's plan

Dance in the infinite space of the subconscious
Move to the beat of the spirit inside
Let go and wade in the healing waters
Let the love be your guide
Open your heart wide

Wake to the reality that you manifest
In this plane we must advance our soul
You will find it once you seek it
Believe it
And achieve it

Sunshine

The sun emerges over the hill
I watch as I rest my coffee on the window sill
The glow enters my eyes and the sunshine hits my face
Another day that God has given me, with grace

Off to my job I venture out
Never knowing what my day may be about
On the drive, I give thanks with gratitude and prayer
Forever knowing you will always be there

As my days goes on, I notice you all around
I can hear your will being done, without a sound
I see you at work, in people I meet
I can see your greatness, in the meek

I do my job and help spread love to all
To lift the ones who may need help standing tall
To be there for the voiceless that may be hurt
Giving them clothes, when they just need a shirt

I venture home on the road I had come
Dancing in my head, to the beat of the drum

Meditating on the day I had
Excited to go home to be a dad

The smile of my first born could melt dry ice
My little girl, with all her sugar and spice
My beautiful wife and lovely home
This is where I find my Ohm

We watch as the sun evades the moon
Knowing our day will be over soon
Off to bed we give thanks and pray
Knowing the sun will be back for another day

I close my eyes and open my mind
And a different world I begin to find
My soul takes flight as my body sleeps
Reminding me that possessions on earth, are not for keeps

We will someday go back to this place of bliss
A place our souls must really miss
Until our time on earth is done
We will wake to another day and another beautiful sun

I Am Affirmations

I am healthy
I am wealthy
I am whole
I am a human body with a happy soul
I am blessed
I am the best
I am wise
I am a beautiful soul in God's eyes
I am strong
I am a beautiful song
I am brilliant
I am respectful, patient, and very resilient
I am kind
I am a great mind
I am smart
I am a loving person with a huge heart
I am caring
I am always sharing
I am love
I am given the words from up above
I am healed
I am an energy field
I am present
I am always doing exactly what is meant

I am alive
I am able to survive
I am protected
I am at one with the universe that's all connected

Change Your Thoughts

Your mind is the engine that moves your reality

Changing your thoughts to success is the real key

Carry no justified resentment

Change your thoughts to love and contentment

Treasure the divinity you have with the One

Change your thoughts before they've even begun

Give up your personal history

Change your thoughts to unlock the universal mystery

Open your mind and become detached

Change your thoughts and let the hole inside be patched

Be open to everything and show love

Change your thoughts and let the divine shine from above

Get quiet and let the universe guide you

Change your thoughts and don't allow them to divide you

Give compassion to all, because you never know

Change your thoughts and let your love light show

Start to think you already have what you need

Change your thoughts to helping others, if you want to succeed

Change your thoughts, change your thoughts

Change your thoughts, from having nothing, to having lots

It Is

I do not mind what will happen

Take me on this life's ride, while I strap in

This too shall pass

Just sit and watch a blade of grass

You don't say?

Don't let the ego lead you astray

I am what I am

Doesn't mean I don't give a damn

Let it all go

Watch as the abundance starts to flow

Forgive and forget

You owe yourself this great debt

Live and let live

If you want, you must give

It is what it is

And will always be for her and his

Forgiveness

Life energy and love come from forgiving
Forgetting the past, taking in that sweet breath of living
Don't let the energy get tangled up inside
Stay in the present and enjoy the current, joyous, ride
Forgiveness is for you, and only you
Start the purge and change your tone too
To a frequency of higher healing
Let your mind change the way you've been feeling
Your thoughts control how you feel
Your mind's the engine, your body the wheel
How much better would you feel if you let things go
Let yourself heal and begin to glow
Forget the past, it's done and gone
With the passing of the day, comes a new dawn
Enjoy the sunlight and the bright starry night
And keep your sight, on doing what's right
Learn from the past and plan for what's ahead
Forgive one another and let kind words be said

Enjoy good thoughts, to enjoy good health
Come to find, life on earth's joyous wealth
The choice is yours and your alone
Forgive, just as Jesus has already shown

Lights

I reach out to you as you fade away
Running out of the breath, needed to stay
The light slips from your eyes
Away it floats as I say my goodbyes

I watch as the breath you breathe, turns into cries
As I watch the light slips into your eyes
I reach out to hold you
Gazing into your ocean eyes of blue

The light can fade and shine so bright
Where does it go when it's out of sight?
How does it survive the darkness of night?
Is a dark light or is it a bright white?

Some say they see the light at the end of a tunnel
Acting as an inter-dimensional funnel
Leading to the unknown
To be held by God, and eventually shown

Shown the true lights
Shown all the colors, for our minds to enjoy the sights
Lights of knowledge so pure

Leaving behind all the pain, you had to endure

The light wants you to have no fear
Glowing bright as if to say, I'm right here
Wanting and waiting for you
Until your time is overdue

Brighten your light, while you can
Be a better person to your fellow man
Think of others and brighten their light
Because you never know when yours will be out
of sight

Trauma

Heartache and pain stuffed deep down inside

Taking you on a physical and emotional ride

The ups and downs, the round and rounds

Blocking out our worldly peaceful sounds

Taking the innocence once given to you

But is it gone or is it being blocked out too?

We take things that were done and send them deep

Deep into the subconscious where it does anything but sleep

Here it orchestrates how you react to daily routine

Forcing the conscious mind to paint a tainted scene

This part of the mind is powerful and weak

It soaks in the good, the bad, the great and the meek

To heal as a person, one must heal the memory that persists

Break the chains that have handcuffed one's mental wrists

Alter the memory and change the mental outcome

And watch as the subconscious will have to succumb

Medications only put a Band-Aid on an open wound

When it's your mind that needs to be retuned

When we start to treat this part of the brain

We will have nothing to lose and everything to gain.

Fear Not to Love

Love dwells in the depth of all

It exudes from every inch of this worldly ball

Fear is keeping the love from getting to you

Block out the fear and let the love shine through

Increase your awareness and focus on love

Let fear go and let love rain down from above

Bad news, media lies, and dis-ease

Fear of death, war, disease

Don't get trapped by the egoic woes

Seek out the good, where the loves just flows

Love doesn't wage wars, it doesn't take advantage

Fear does this and it's something we must manage

Virtue and wisdom are two weapons we possess

Patience and compassion are ours to access

Let love win the battles that we must wage

Allow it to be the main character, up on our stage

Open the heart and close the mind

Dissolve the fear with love, and just be kind

His Will

You walked into my world that day
With the biggest smile that the world couldn't hide in any way
When you spoke, the words rolled from your tongue with ease
And your scent swept over me like a summer breeze
Your hair looked like crop of majestic willows
Your deep green and brown eyes, like two comfy pillows
Body sculpted like a piece of art
Our hearts linked so tight, nothing could pull it apart
Your soul and mine, danced while we slept
Telling secrets in dreams that our minds kept
Our auras combined to shine like the light of the sun
On that day we wed, two became one
Life fills your body, after our bodies combine
God then picked a soul from his vast divine
We prayed for health and God answered that prayer
The day she came, all I could do was stare
Two became three and our lives changed forever

Wanting to nourish her every life endeavor
Now we sit, watch, and pray
Watch as you change from day to day
Your tiny cries turn to belly laughs
We only see the change when we look at photographs
Hair that seems to never end
Big blues eyes, with just a glance, all hearts will mend
Your charismatic ways, and stubborn will
Your life's destiny, we know you will fulfill
We sit at night to thank God for what we have been given
To help us to continue to be driven
To help mankind and change this worldly dimension
And remember to have nothing but good intention
We pray as though it already is
Because we know that our will is His.

I Am

I am what
Am I this
Am I that
I am bliss

I am who
Am I we
Am I you
I am thee

I am when
Am I now
Am I sin
I am how

I am them
Am I me
Am I numb
I am she

I am him
Am I then
Am I dim
I am zen

I am ego
Am I all
Am I placebo
I am tall

I am that
Am I just
Am I spat
I am dust

I am thee
Am I you
Am I free
I am too

I am god
Am I all
Am I flawed

True Dreams

Ask and you shall receive

But when you ask you must believe

Hold no judgment of good or bad

And ask as if it is something, you already have had

Combine the feeling of the wish with knowing

That's when your manifestation will truly start showing

Speak the language the universe can hear

Talk with your heart without hidden motives or fear

Let the vibrational words flow out of you

And watch as all your dreams come true

Do not ask with your physical voice

But surround yourself with this manifesting choice

Dream as if it is a present fact

And assume it true and forever intact

The universe listens when you ask this way

So, what are you going to manifest today?

Bad and Good

I stood underneath a skyscraper today
Could barely see the top
I watched as a great sequoia tree began to sway
Hoping it would never drop

I watched as the freeways filled
Wasting away another perfect day
I sat and watched as a banana was peeled
By a gorilla showing its young the way

I looked out the window during my flight
I saw cancerous city growth evading the land
A waterfall hitting the river below was a beautiful sight
As I feel the mist caress my hand

I walk into a prison full of men
Feeling the pain surrounding my soul
I look at the pyramids and wonder when
Will this world ever again be whole

Watching the smoke roll in from the fires
Seeing the scar left in its path
The green grass grows tall with healthy desires

Cleansing the earth of our worldly wrath

I see plastic in the carcass of a dead whale
And watch as my tears hit the sand
Watching as a cleansing vessel sets sail
Wishing I could lend a hand

I see fast food, cheap thrills, and expensive things
And I try to show my daughter the right way
I see the spiritual awakening and the gifts God brings
We all see Bad and Good, but we must remember to pray.

Breath Deep

If we hold onto our breath, we will surely pass away

This a truth that we must all obey

Breath was given to our bodies made of star dust

By Source, who has given us life, with trust

When we focus on our breath, we connect to our soul

Doing this lets our mind, body, spirit become whole

We cannot hold onto our breath forever

But we can release with it, our anger, resentment, and fear however

Allow the shame, hostility, and pain

To flow out of you like an open drain

Breathe in all that holy inspiration

Breathe out with a lifegiving transformation

The mind will transcend the grasps of the ego

Lifting high into the sky like a soaring eagle

Raising its arms from the depth of our deepest sea

To receive the love from above and change the I to we

Does not everything need to breath to survive?

Does this not connect us all and make us all alive?

When we realize that the connection is only a breath away

We will then breathe deep and give thanks someday.

Patience

Through patience we learn to know ourselves
It teaches us to take our desires and put them on an imaginary shelf
Patience tests and measures our ideals
Helps us to use our faith, while our worldly need heals

It gives us time to understand through virtue
It'll shake you down and really search you

It makes us embrace all of our spiritual attributes
Showing our desires as time needy prostitutes

In patience possess ye your soul
Elevating our evolutionary role

Patience is a skill that one needs to constantly nurture
Changing who you are and altering who you were

Patience occurs between experience and reaction
And how we handle situations, with or without satisfaction

Patience with oneself, life, or one another
Are all obstacles, like a fire you must smother

Cultivate less stress, anxiety, and frustration
Enjoy your time, as you wait at that bus station

Find the joy in the challenges this life may bring
Turn the noise into a song that you sing

Change the wait, to a time of rest
Take the change, and give it your best

Walk away from instant gratification
And let the universe be your daily validation

Remain still, in the midst of disappointment
Then use your patience, as a worry killing ointment

When you figure this aspect of life out
You will be living the dream, without a doubt

Hold On

Life's is going to teach us a lot

It already has and still look at all we've got

It's going to hurt right down to our very core of existence

And we're going to fight that feeling with all of our resistance

It's going to be joyful to the point that we don't want that to leave

And it's going to be scarier than we could ever believe

I may not know whether I'm right or wrong

But with you I hope that I will always belong

If we can just hold on through the tough days ahead

And remember those words on the day that we wed

I know our life will be showered with a lot more joy

And that's something I just cannot destroy

We're going to fight and not agree

But the best thing about that is that it will be we

Not I, or you, but us

Building this life surrounded by trust

I want you know how much I care for you

And I hope you know how much I love you too.

Together we're better, apart we're not

I'd be a rich man, if you were all I got.

Love you

Alcohol

Deceptive and smooth with a kick

Igniting a flame inside with a gasoline wick

Dampening souls and dimming the light

Taking away our very human right

Opening up channels to allow things in

Which bring unknowingly ungodly sin

Tormenting the very essence of life

And adding to all of the pain and strife

Crippling the ability to engage

Bringing out inner demons with outer rage

Starving comprehension of this beautiful surrounding

Only to leave humanity cold, shaky, with heads pounding

Lusting for more once the effects leave

Which set us up for failure, pain, and disease

Drain our wealth and create rifts with friends

Waking up always trying to make amends

Emptying a bottle to feel empty inside

Only to fill that bottle with the tears that have been cried

Away I Lift

I saw a bird flying today
Watched it, until it was too far away
Wished I could hitch a ride
Take me away to the other side
Let me feel the freedoms above
Riding the waves of infinite love

I went to the ocean and sat today
Wishing the currents would carry my pain away
Take the issues and wash them clean
Show me things, never before seen
Cleanse the soul, enrich my heart
Find the hurt and tear it apart

I sit on a mountain and watch the sunrise
Through the colors, I saw your eyes
Beautiful blues with shades of green
Prettiest eyes, I'd ever seen
They starred deep into my very being
I closed my eyes but kept on seeing

I laid in the sand of the desert tonight
I looked up to see the light so bright
The stars peered deep within

Almost to admire my worldly sin
I smiled back and gave a grin
Because I know, that we will meet again

I laid in bed and closed my eyes
Another world appeared to my surprise
A gift was given to me that night
From there on my soul was able to take flight
The colors were all so vivid and bright
I found myself immersed in different shades of light.

My waking self is my dreamer's dream
My sleeping self is the new reality, it may seem
The bird flying, is an attainable gift
The ocean waters, begin to shift
The mountain sunrise, is a guitar rift
Where I lay in the desert, away I lift.

Grow Slow

You entered this world with closed eyes
Now they're open and everything's a surprise

The colors of the trees, as they turn to fall
or the colored crayons you use, to write on the wall

We rock you to bed and sing you songs
As we rock, we try and take away your wrongs

We put you down gently, now sleep tight
And we say a little prayer, before we kiss you good night

You wake up ready to explore the day
"Come get me, Mommy, Daddy," I hear you say

You gather your blankets and teddy bear
And away we go to our bed to share

Off to school you go to learn and play
Doing things your very own special way

Meeting new people and learning rules

Makings friends with all the boys and girls

You love to play tag and hide and seek
Sometimes you trip and scrape your cheek

You say, "I'm okay," get back up and go
You're one tough kid, that we know

You're learning quick with numbers and words
You know all the insects, reptiles, and birds

You sing the songs we sing at night
You're even learning how to read and write

We wish you'd slow down and stay small for a bit
Although we can't wait to buy you a baseball mitt

For now, we can go and play in the park
And wish for sun, until it gives way to the dark

At night we give thanks for the day that we had
And you give hugs and kisses to Mom and Dad

Gather your blankets and teddy bear
To go bed loved with compassion and care

Ni-night little angel, have a good sleep
As you lay there hugging your favorite sheep

We can't wait to see what your life will bring
But please grow slow and enjoy everything.

I Love You God

I love you God, I love you God, I love you God I say

In my mind and out loud every day

I use this phrase in times of need

I use it in my life when I want to succeed

It's used in times to take away all fear

This prayer can be used every day, month, and year

For anything, at anytime

For any reason or any rhyme

He hears you because he is part of you

So, when you say or think "I love you God" you're talking to yourself too

Use it to help guide you when you've strayed your path

Say it and know we have a loving God, who delivers no wrath

If you believe that he loves you back, just the same

And that he's saying I love you too, you're ahead of the game

It's a simple prayer, but a strong one

Use it and enjoy your life in the long run

Right before your eyes, things manifest

God hears all and for you he wants what's best

Source has put you here to experience life through you

He has said I love you from day one, so say I love you too

Reality

The reality that we live in is a reflection of our own thoughts

If we think bad ideas of ourselves, we will watch as our body rots

While we manifest the three-dimensional world around us

We must hold on and wait until our true selves have found us

We will then start to think more loving

And stop with the mental pushing and shoving

Allow the world to be created through the thoughts of love

And watch as the heavens come to earth from above

Start to think thoughts of greatness and joy

And create a loving environment for a girl or a boy

Heal the subconscious mind and change your perception

Give yourself a chance for your own resurrection

They say people don't change, but people talk a lot

The reality is, you can do anything that your mind has sought

All around you there are various forms of what's real

But we are limited to the bodies senses that God has given us to feel

A tree to us is quite different from a tree to an ant

Or a tree to a bird is not just a plant

Reality is the perception of the being you are

But you must know that you can change your reality and raise the bar

Start to think better of yourself

And watch as your physical beings manifests its own health

Think good thoughts of the people in your life

And watch the change in a husband or wife

Give hopeful ideas to your child's days from birth

And watch them flourish during their time on earth

Think thoughts of abundance and wealth

And give thanks to everything that's been given oneself

Say the world is changing for the better and believe it

Only then will mankind be able to achieve it

Thoughts are more powerful than we ever knew possible

Good thoughts will help us cross oceans thought to be uncrossable

Reality is exactly what you choose to make it

So, take your old way of thinking and choose to break it

We are a loving, caring, strong, healthy mankind

And this is something the world will soon find

Staying Awake

Staying awake, is staying the path to enlightenment

It's like tuning your soul, thriving to brighten it

Like staring at a dark night and being able to see the light in it

Or testing a tied knot, only to further tighten it

Recognize your events for what they are

Synchronicities are not at all bizarre

And let the universe guide you from afar

In this vastness of light energy, you are a star

Life is better when we stay awake

We start to realize what is and isn't fake

That our purpose on earth is for God's sake

And that it wouldn't be much of an experience, if it were a piece of cake

It's easy to fall back into the third dimension

And forget about your upcoming spiritual ascension

But it'll be harder to enjoy if you don't pay attention

Making your life here much harder, not to mention

Practice compassion and love

And continue to listen to the inner words from above

That inner knowing, that has always been spoken of

Let the words of God give you that needed shove
Get in a routine and stay the course

Allow yourself to float in this universal life force

Look at our current worldly views and have remorse

This is a life that God surely will endorse

Remember how you got to where you are

Put all those events on your desk, in a jar

To remind you of your progress in this lifetime so far

And know that you can't heal an old wound, without accepting the scar

Just for You

In my meditation today I stood upon a mountain with Jesus

He told me that God created this for every man just to please us

Everything was created for everyone

From the glowing moon to the shining sun

To the flowing oceans and mountains high

The smallest flowers, to the trees that seem to touch the sky

He told me that the world was created just for you

The air was yours and the water was too

The birds sang for your very own delight

And the snow was for you, beautiful, cold, and white

Mother Earth was a gift that holds all that you need

Like its healing plants with abundant seed

Its life giving air and life giving food

Or its life giving love through vibrational mood

Source gave us instruments to express our own emotion

Mankind's emotion can highly relate to our physical ocean

Churning, ever changing, and vast

Forgiving, supporting, showing signs of a past

Jesus held my hand and asked why would man hurt this gift

I sat there wondering as I watched him leave in a far off drift

Mother Earth is a onetime gift from God

And a marvel that we should certainly applaud

But we must be better at co creating this land

You have the power right there in your hand

Treat Mother Earth right and she'll be good to you

Let the generations after us have a sky that is blue

I thanked Jesus for showing me this

And I started back down the mountain to our worldly bliss.

What if I said the moon knew your name

And the stars knew you, just the same

You matter in this vast collection of energy and light

And your actions matter, so show thanks and make your actions right

Meditation

Close your eyes, open your mind

Let go of fear and unwind

Release your innermost ideas that are thought

Forget all worldly ideals that are taught

Find your higher self

May it lead you to prosperity, love, and wealth

Health and happiness are a state of mind

That is easily obtained and are never silver lined

Go to a place that's free of negativity

Love is here with blissful productivity

It is a place without any doubt

Find your true self inside and let it out

Everything we are, is what we think

Our subconscious thinking is the missing link

Change your personal views of life

And rid your body of painful strife

Meditation is a form of medication

Communication that will heal the nation

Up your vibration and enjoy your physical formation

We are a generation that needs this education

Do some investigation and see a transformation
Healing shows no discrimination

Just needs the mind to allow for activation

Abundance

Invite unlimited abundance into your life

Cut the tension of depravity like a knife

Tap into the subconscious mind

And let the free flow of abundant life unwind

Let go of all things learned

In your mind those things have been burned

Get into yourself and release you inner knowing

Going within is like a finding a seed that needs sowing

Get connected to the universe around you

And these knew understandings will astound you

Be open to change and embrace it

Take the hate inside of you and displace it

Soften the thinking mind and let the higher self-speak

That's when the flow of abundance will peak

Focus on what you want to attract into your being

Close your eyes, quiet the mind, and start seeing.

Changes

Wake from a dream and ponder your thoughts

Was the dream a reality of haves or have nots

Is your dreaming self having a dream played out?

Is this dream your dreaming a dream no doubt?

See our dreams are a reflection of our subconscious mind

In another dimension of space and time

Use those dreams to help with your daily play

Alter your reality with that knowledge today

Change your lives with your mind

Do your part to ensure good for all mankind

The lives we live and have lived and are living

Ensure our souls' growth so start self-forgiving

Bleed away the doctrines of fear

And know the universe will always be here

To love and protect you at all times

And to shelter you from your ego's hellish crimes

Changes come when you least expect them

But they come from within, so let your conscious resurrect them

We all have powers that we learned to fear

Religion has helped to keep you here

God would never hold fear over your head

His loving gentle being, wants all of your fear to be dead

So, I ask that you change

Open up, and let your life rearrange

Let the man's ego keep you in the dark no longer

Move to the light, sit, wait, and ponder.

Judgment

To cast negative thoughts on others

Is no way to treat our sisters and brothers

We all are trying our best in these lives we live

A little bit of encouragement and love is so easy to give

Try to put on their shoes and walk their steps

Really see why they are down there in the depths

Raise their vibrations and enhance their light

It will change a dull black to a bright white

Open your soul and invite in love

Give compassion and rise above

You're too proud, humble yourself

Compassion and love are the soul's money and wealth

Give thanks and live free

Run away from all negativity

Swallow your pride and look inside

And think about how you'd like to be treated in the life's ride

5:55

Woke up this morning and looked at my phone

5:55, I know it's Jesus, guiding me until I come home

Get up, get dressed, and go downstairs

Made my food and think of my nighttime prayers

As I dream, I am in another dimension and time

My own manifested place, not without reason or rhyme

But quite opposite in all actuality

Dreams are just a different form of our own daily reality

I bring coffee to my beautiful wife

Look at our baby monitor and am thankful for my beautiful life

I feed my dogs and pack nourishment for the day

Hop in my car and begin this daily game we play

The scene this morning was that of orchestrated bliss

A sunrise that even the blind couldn't miss

The sun peeked over the hills and shot beams of gold

And as I drove, I watched as a new day began to unfold

I wondered what the spirit guides had in store for me

As I wonder, I trust, and I wait patiently

Nothing in life happens without reason

A tragedy is a chance to change a new season

Take the bad and look for the good it may bring
And down from the heavens the gifts of good will ring

Trust in yourself and your inner knowing

Be a good person, help others, and keep that smiling glowing

Bring people up and watch as you make a change

Think good thoughts and watch as your world will rearrange.

Today I woke up at 5:55

And I have never, ever, felt so alive.

Mother Spirt Ayahuasca

Ayahuasca the tool to enhance your life
To rid the subconscious of pain and strife
Mother Aya, the loving, nurturing, healing being
She takes you out of the darkness and into the seeing
Seeing the past and wrongs that have been done
She heals all parts and brings them back to one
Mother shows you things you may not have known
Mother helps you grow in places you may not have grown
She cradles you while she mends your mind
because without sound mind you get stuck in place or time
Present time is the place to be
And without healing the past it's a time that's impossible to see
Mother will give you exactly what you need
she will chew up and toss you around until you are freed
Freed from the past and freed from yourself
taking painful memories, knocking them off your subconscious shelf
Not only will you be able heal the mind

but also, the physical pains she is able to find
The pain of injury doesn't stand in her way
She sheds light on the body to help you manifest a new day
Spiritually, she shows you that you need not fear
The universe, God, spirits, angels, will always be here
There is no discrimination of prior wrongs
Taking screams and sorrowing cries and turning them to songs
Giving light to the connection of everything we are
From the tiniest atom to the biggest, brightest star
You Shamans are showing the world how to really heal
Helping the numb, to once again feel
The trickle effect that you're having on this earth
Will change countless lives from the days of their birth
You healers are giving life to people that have been dead
In hell on earth which lies in the head
There is no hell, only the ones we create
Drink in the love, sit back, and wait

I write you this poem to express my love for what you're doing
I pray for more healings to come and keep up that good brewing!

Music

When it hits you feel no pain

Piercing your ears and into your brain

Sending joyous vibrations throughout your being

Music can paint you a picture that does not need seeing

It brightens your mood and enhances your life

Helps to heal a wounded heart's pain and strife

Can tell a story of a time or place

Brings together and unites the human race

It stands up for one's belief

And can give the soul some needed relief

Lay by the ocean and listen to mother earth sing

Sit in the mountains and listen to a cold fresh spring

Lay quiet under the stars above

And let the universe sing out its love

Dance to the music of a child's laughter

And embrace the feelings you get thereafter

March to the tone of your inner being

The music within is beautifully made and freeing

Let birds sing you a song through the quiet after a morning rain

And feel their loving tones enter your brain

Sit quiet in the desert late at night

Close your eyes and let your ears be your sight

Listen to wolves sing out to the moon

Chasing it across the sky with a magic tune

Go deep into the forest and you can hear the plants grow

The buzz of insects will make your heart glow

The sound the ice makes as the glaciers grind

Is a vibration from Mother Earth's own divine mind

The sun sends us music in the form of light

Breathing musical life into this world so bright

I can't wait to hear the tones of heaven above

Sounds of then and now of what is and once was

Everything is energy and music is too

That is why it resonates with you

Music is everywhere vibrating around us

If we stop to listen, it can surely astound us

Love

Love is an experience of eternal infinity

Surrounding us in holy divinity

When you find it, you will know

It's a never-ending ecstasy flow

Love is your entire being

Love isn't blind, but it is seeing

Love penetrates deep within

Love is where death ends, and life begins

You can find it in many different forms

In a gentle breezy day or in turbulent windy storms

In a child's smile or an old man's grin

In a great loss or a joyous win
Love is warm, love is kind

Love is out there and easy to find

The air we breathe was given in love

To help us breathe until we go above

The food we eat, the water we drink

The songs we hear and the lyrics that make you think

Love is the prayers that are spoken

Love is helping your loved ones to be woken

Love can heal, love can save

Love is riding on a beautiful frequency wave

Love is yours and love is mine

Love is given to us from the one divine.

We all deserve love and are able to give it

The question is, are you are able to live it?

Collective Consciousness Shift

Prayer, meditation, co-creations

Loving, caring, raising vibrations

Controlling and focusing our emotion

Activating our collective consciousness magic potion

Two negatives can't create a positive

Love for your enemies, is all you should give

May we join to change our present physical reality

By collectively meditating on respect for duality

Start using our co-creative consciousness in our favor

Get our powers back and never waver

Stop allowing our minds to be dragged down

Go into Mother Nature, put your bare feet on the ground

They want us to be a collective cripple

Throw a stone of love in the pond of life and watch it ripple

Love Inspired

Love connects us to one another

Unconditionally tying us to every sister, brother, father, mother

Leaving no spaces separated

With no room for conditional hatred

Bonding every being together to the infinite one

To connect with the LOVE consciousness, we shall run

Forgiving all with empathic smiles

Lighting all eyes with love, for miles and miles

Sharing kind words and uplifting thoughts

Encouraging others, to encourages others, a lot

Welcoming others into your home, who have not

Giving of yourself, even when you think you cannot

Looking to those who our Lord God has brought

On this earth, their wisdom will be taught

Treat your neighbor, as you want to be treated

Leave unconsciousness and hatred justly defeated

Love is the one and only answer to all

Let the love shower upon you like peaceful rainfall.

Sedona

No expectations, just a destination,

Sedona, the land of manifestation,

A group of people with a will to change,

A place where there really is no strange,

Likeminded people coming together as one,

To do some work and have some fun,

Kim with her aura that takes up the room,

And Tye who may have flown in on a magical broom,

Here to guide us toward what we all need,

To collapse the old, and plant a new seed,

Live channeling, helped some to let go,

Numerology helped us to look inside to know,
Hikes in the mountains grounded us to Mother Earth,

And a new conscious connecting started to give birth,

The peace park was a place the world should be,

Where prayer flags fly and the hate set free,

Rajulio and the heat, melted away years of doubt,

Giving it to the fire and shouting it out,

Vibrating sounds from the musical bath,

Gave our third eyes a trip down a beautiful path,

Words can't express Astarius Miraculi,

It was as if he were a gift that came from the sky,

Angel valley is an angelic wonderland,

It's like walking around on God's right hand,

With my doubts laid to rest and my heart full,

I can go home now with a cleansed soul.

Akashic Record

Words flow out of me like the stream of
consciousness that surround us

The ever-flowing knowledge of all, that has
always been around us

Some are able to tap into this sea of then, now,
and yet to come

And most others wade through its vastness going
to and from

The source of this ever-changing sea

Is a beautiful mixture of what is, what has been,
and what is soon to be

We created its contents with our free will

Splashing around in a space that we will never fill

Leaving all pieces of us along the way

That will eventually be looked back upon some day

Or some night or some space in time

In some melody, song, or in some rhyme

It may be downloaded into us at times of need

It may be transmitted as a life-giving seed

Inspired inspirations that the spirits give us

Forever showing that God will always forgive us

Letting us, let him, experience our very being

To advance our soul from blind, to seeing

To climb the mountains and cross the seas

Stand tall and fight, only to get down on our knees

In the Bible, the book of life it's called

The akashic records is there for all to be enthralled

Tap in and gain the knowing

Ask God, put out the intention, and watch as the
Source starts the showing

Death

Death comes in times least expected

To the worst people and the most respected

Other times death is around the corner for a while

Leaving an emotional path as long as the Nile

Sometimes is comes right at birth

And the young helpless child never sees earth

Others live for many years

Sharing smiles, frowns, laughter, and tears

They say that the good die young

But I think that they don't leave earth until their purpose is done

Until they have touched the lives of strangers, family, and friends

Up the stairs of heaven, the soul ascends

Death only ends our time on earth

Take it for what it is and for what it's worth

Some die peacefully but we all exist forever

They may be gone now but forgotten never

Don't feel bad for the ones that have passed

The place that they are now is far more vast

It's hard on everyone when a loved one dies

No one ever likes to say goodbyes

There's faith and hope to meet again someday

Maybe not tomorrow or today

But some day down the line when it's your time

Up the stairs of heaven, you'll make that climb

And at the top your loved ones will be

With arms wide open, waiting patiently

Here there are no more tears, sorrow, crying, or pain

with nothing to lose and everything to gain

God gives us hope, peace, and rest

Everlasting happiness and only the best

As our loved ones leave this place

Know that the rest of their soul family is waiting, with a warm embrace.

Death is only the soul's rebirth

There's far more out there than this three-dimensional earth

Changes

Why is change so hard?
Everyone wants bigger, better, faster, stronger
Why wait for crisis, disease, betrayal?
Make the change and let it affect you no longer

You can change in a state of pain
Or in a state of joy and inspiration
Don't wait for a tragedy to change
Be proactive about your new revelation

When you have the same thoughts
You make the same choices
Leading to the same actions
You then experience the same mental voices

Then those voices lead to the same experience
Producing the same emotions
Leading to the same thoughts
That churn in your head like the oceans

How you think, act, and feel, makes up you
And this is what creates your reality
If you keep thinking the same thoughts
Then your thoughts, you shall be

If you're not using your thoughts
To embark on a new life goal
You'll be stuck with memories of your past
Becoming a predictable person, easy to control

When you start thinking about problems
You're living in the past
If your thoughts create your future
Then your problems will always last

Are your memories of the past even real?
Memory is creative and your brain changes
Don't embellish the experience to enhance the emotion
Alter and accept the memory, that's what change is

The repetitive cycle gives the mind to the body
Making it reproduce the past from your thought
You crave the predictable future
Losing a fight, before it's fought

You reach for Facebook, Instagram, and Twitter
To connect with the familiar in your known reality
Performing unconscious events to feel
Creating a habit where your mind can flee

You blame others for your present
But are you ever even there?
To be present is the space to reach
Presence is the mind becoming aware

Don't lose your free will to a program
Let your personality create your personal reality
Get yourself back from your surroundings
Start to be the you, you're meant to be

Don't be a victim of the conditions of your environment
Believe in your future today
As if it were already happening
Change your thoughts, change your life, it's the only way

To change is to be greater than time
Don't live in the familiar past, the known
Don't live in the predictable future, the known
Get into that sweet spot, the present time zone

MLK Dreams a dream

In 1963 they marched on Washington DC

With life, liberty and the pursuit of happiness, as their decree

To cash a check for freedom for all

And collectively watch the divisions of mankind fall

Not to be guilty of wrongful deeds

To have a dream of freedom to meet all persons' needs

Not to drink from the cup of bitterness and hatred

But to use the soul force inside that we all hold sacred

To march ahead and do not turn back

Stop seeing color as just yellow, brown, white, or black

Not to wallow in the valley of despair

Because ALL mankind is created equal, as free as the air

Let one be judged by the content of their character

Join hands as sisters and brothers, in the great land of America

Let freedom reign from coast to coast

Let love be the answer, first and foremost

Dreams come true when you feel them in your heart

Unite as one in this dream and do your part

We all lose if Martin Luther King Junior's dream dies

So, feel this dream in your heart tonight, as you close your eyes

One

Infinite oneness evading space and time

Ever connected in this ever-changing paradigm

Blossoming from the dust of the cosmic web of all

Expressing itself through an intelligent energy ball

Manifesting light in frequency form

Vibrating from a miraculous energy storm

Endless possibilities flow out and back in

An energy that ends where it once would begin

Spinning itself outward to be undone

To regain its magnificence again as one

Love and Light

The light beckons to be seen through the dark

Racing at a fast pace, to reach its mark

Penetrating the empty space between

Consistently yearning for itself to be seen

Love is waiting in the depths of us all

To be given the chance to passionately enthrall

To share itself through the law of one

Until the notion of separation is undone

Be the light that shines so bright

That you brighten others from black to white

May the glow vibrate into eternal infinity

Shining up, into the holy divinity

Let love heal all past wrongs

Let love change those wrongs to beautiful songs

Dance and sing them out loud with bliss

It was meant to happen and deep down you know this

Shine the light on the path of the present

Stay focused on your spiritual ascent

Glow with the knowledge you have been bestowed

Enjoying the downs and ups along your road

Love the light that your spirit exudes

Let the love and light brighten your moods

Give the love and light, given to you, right back

Then the love and light you will never lack.

Life Ripple

Be the rock that creates the ripple

Watch the love flow out double, then triple

Don't hesitate to be a positive light

The love you express will always be right

People will not look down on you for it

Because deep down they know it's legit

We all want to express ourselves and be heard

So give a smile, a hello, a kind word

Judgment only comes from one's own inner turmoil

Plant the seed of love in the subconscious soil

Wake Up

What are you doing to prevent the hate?

Watching the news, complaining about your state?

Blaming the so-called "opposition"

If you haven't heard of the Hegelian Dialectic, there's something you're missing

Don't be a pawn in the chess board game of life

We all know that pawns, become the king's sacrifice

Be the bridge of love to your neighbor

Bite into the apple of knowledge and savor the flavor

The things we should know, aren't taught to us

But if we seek it out, it will be brought to us

What if countries didn't have a name

Who would we be at war with, who takes all the blame?

They would be people like you and I

Who come from the same creator of the utmost high

Religion, politics, news, war

Alcohol, drugs, rich and poor

Keeping you right there, in your place

So they can sit back and dominate the human race

But they can't dominate what lies inside

Look deep within, and enjoy that loving ride

If we all stop getting programmed by the news

And stop feeding on their collective point of views

Stop being addicted to violence and hate

Rid your body of cortisol, so that it can start to create

Let us grasp that strong collective feeling of love

So that no war on earth could ever rise above

Be the change you want to see

And stop being the person you think they want you to be

Be Grey

We're told to strive toward the light

But without the dark, it's out of sight

Balancing one another in this dimension

Helping to evolve ourselves though this comprehension

Through pain, we understand joy

And to create, we must also destroy

Wrong and right are at the ends of polarity

Ever expanding our wisdom and clarity

The devil and angel work side by side

To show you a glimpse of each other, on this life's ride

Positive and negative, are experience

And if the lesson is not learned, there's a reoccurrence

Grey is the spot of neutrality, between the dark and light

A place we can sit without judgment, of what's wrong or right

A neutral zone

With a mixture of frequency expressed through a grey tone

When you chase the light, your shadow grows

And when you chase the dark, the light always knows

Gain this wisdom and see both with the prospective of love

The light and dark are within, not somewhere below or above

Find your calm in a neutrality expressed though a centered grey

And enjoy your role in this illusion of life, in this beautiful game we play

Remove the Veil

Vision does not always allow you to see

An awakened blind person, can see perfectly

You can decipher the message hidden beneath

You can believe the truth, without a belief

We cannot stop the ripple of a pond with our hand

But we can see through glass, that was once sand

Don't deny yourself from your own spiritual intelligent intuition

See beyond, the past intentional conditioning apparition

Recognize your own synchronicity

A clue from the universe's own authenticity

Connect the dots that keep being shown to you

Let omnipresent divine light shine on through

Don't ignore the infinite intelligence that presents

In this three-dimensional reality of events

There's more to life than what you're taught

Open to the possibilities, that you have not

Eternity is now, has been, and will always be

Remove the veil so that you might see

Mind's Eye

We come into this world with spiritual amnesia

And it's our job to cleanse the mind of this mental anesthesia

Sent down from the stars to expand our souls

Awaken in this life, to fill in the holes

You may not recall, but you chose your lessons

And without these lessons, there'd be no blessings

You must have the dark to see the light

We've allowed for division, now it's time to unite

ALL religions are a pathway to God

For the omnipresent, INFINITE Creator, to have one path, would be quite odd

He wouldn't give you free will, then show you his wrath

Learn from your lessons and get back on the right path

Discern everything with what resonates deep within

Within, is where you should always begin

Do the healing, start the revealing

Feel the feeling, and get back the power that the world's been stealing

Advance yourself in this life that's a game

In this illusion we play, for such a short-time frame

You're living in eternity

In this three-dimensional world until our souls reach maturity

It's not game over, once you die

Meditate on that, and open your mind's eye

Go Within

All life exists within me

An utter calm within, where my truths are free

Here the glamour of the physical world does not exist

Your own thoughts of divinity, you must enlist

Thoughts of good I accept and evil I ignore

The vast space of my inner world I explore

God, the subconscious universal mind

Has manifested himself though me I find

I reach ever upward and outward to the light

Expanding my knowledge, love, and collective insight

I place my future in divine hands

As I am a grain, in the universal beach of sands

I turn over my problems to the all knowing

I have complete confidence that all circumstances are there for my spiritual growing

The universe seeks to answer my every need, in this reality

As I believe in my heart, so shall it be unto me

There is greatness in my friend and enemy

We are all brothers and sisters seeking the same, in some degree

I open my heart and my mind

Keeping my thoughts in the path of truths of all kind

I am filled with the power and abundance of the love the universe bestows

I put out the intention and watch as my beautiful life flows

Wake up

Are we going to let everyone do else do all the heavy lifting?
Or are we going to take back what's ours and help with this conscious shifting
Are you going to take the blue pill and stay asleep?
Or take the red pill and dive in deep?
Wake up to the knowledge and see from an openminded perception
Stop believing the lies of the made-man deception
Open your eyes to the reality hidden under your nose
It's time for mankind's truths to become exposed
Tesla had technology to give endless power to all
The walls of hidden knowledge will soon fall
We went to the moon in 1969
And you're telling me that 35 mpg is top of the line?
People keep getting cancer but there's no cure
There's been many cures, and that's for sure
The system is set up to keep you in your place
We're slaves to the elite, are you keeping pace?
Knowledge has been suppressed to help the wealthy
Not many rich people look unhealthy

The history we are taught is a straight up joke
Honestly how much longer can they blow this smoke
To the victor the history is written
To attain the fruit of knowledge, one must risk being snake bitten
The bible has been changed over the course of history
To influence the faithful man to fall in line and to further the mystery
Taking out reincarnation and adding hell was the plan
The Bible decrees that woman must submit to the dominance of man
Well that's finally changing with the awakening movement
When we figure out, we are all one, that'll be an improvement
Big Pharma trying to keep you sick
"Just close your eyes, it's only a prick"
Closing your eyes is the key to their success
Knowledge is what they want to suppress
So, you can go on living in this 3D reality
Or you can open your eyes and start to see
No one's going to drop this information at your door
You must search it out, go explore

Check out people like Alan Watts,
Now that's a guy that will help you connect some dots
Or sign up for Gaia and go down that rabbit hole
Get out of the confines of your comfortable fishbowl
The more you know the more prepared you'll be
When the disclosures come to set us free
Get the knowledge to be able to stand up tall
And remember that love is the answer for all

2020 Visions

2020, the year of perfect vision
What a beautiful time that we are living
To see a shift from taking to giving
Even though the news keeps pushing the division
The dark is being brought to light
The bad actors in this illusion are coming into sight
We are in the midst of a great spiritual fight
Time to pray, meditate, and forget about being wrong or right
As we shift into this new energy of love
We will watch as false idols fall from their positions above
Into the light the darkness dwellers will get a shove
And once healed, their souls will be lifted on the wings of a white dove
2020 the year they pushed to divide
Pushed by their ego's hatred and pride
Only to show their most vulnerable side
Their need for love, that we will most defiantly provide
A spiritual war of biblical proportion
Filling this illusion full of distortion
Ridding the world of human extortion

Saving all life, before the need for abortion
Life after life, will surely come
And back we'll go to the spiritual realm we have come from
A place you surely can't take your worldly income
Where knowledge and love are for all, not just some
The age of Aquarius has finally arrived
An end of the age of Pieces, a time religion survived
But a time when spirituality was deprived
A lost knowing which will be revived
Fifth dimension where awareness is in a balanced state
A golden age of mindfulness is our fait
The boom of technology to bring us up to date
A space faring age, we await
Go within to find the answer and enjoy the ride
Lose the ego and selfish pride
Take in each moment and look on the bright side
Because peace is coming, and it's going to be worldwide!

Made in the USA
Monee, IL
26 May 2021